G000109043

EDITED BY HELEN EXLEY

Published in 2019 by Helen Exley®LONDON in Great Britain.
Illustration by Juliette Clarke © Helen Exley Creative Ltd 2019.
All the words by Pam Brown, Charlotte Gray, Hannah C. Klein, Linda
Gibson, Stuart & Linda Macfarlane, Pamela Dugdale
© Helen Exley Creative Ltd 2019.
Design, selection and arrangement © Helen Exley Creative Ltd 2019.
The moral right of the author has been asserted.

ISBN 978-1-78485-186-6

12 11 10 9 8 7 6 5 4 3 2

OTHER BOOKS IN THE SERIES

Be Happy!   *Be Confident!*   *Be Brave!*
Be Positive!   *Be a Rebel!*

OTHER BOOKS BY HELEN EXLEY

365 Yes to life!   Calm and Mindfulness

Friendship 365   A gift of Happiness   Live! Love! Laugh!

Helen Exley®LONDON
16 Chalk Hill, Watford, Herts WD19 4BG, UK
www.helenexley.com

Be You!

Helen Exley

Always remember
you are braver
than you believe,
stronger than you seem,
and smarter
than you think.

CHRISTOPHER ROBIN

My will shall shape my future.
Whether I fail or succeed
shall be no one's doing but my own.
I am the force;
I can clear any obstacle before me
or I can be lost in the maze.
My choice;
my responsibility;
win or lose,
only I hold the key to my destiny.

ELAINE MAXWELL

Don't compromise yourself. You are all you've got.

JANIS JOPLIN 1943 – 1970

Once you figure out
who you are and what
you love about yourself,
it all kind of
falls into place.

JENNIFER ANISTON, B. 1969

I've finally
stopped running away
from myself.
Who else is there
better to be?

GOLDIE HAWN, B. 1945

You have got to discover you,
what you do, and trust it.

BARBRA STREISAND, B. 1942

Be what you are
– a rare and lovely gem.
But polish, facet,
– bring to life
all that you possess.
Delight the world.

ODILE DORMEUIL

Don't let the noise of others' opinions
drown out your own inner voice.
And most important,
have the courage to follow your heart
and intuition.
They somehow already know
what you truly want to become.

STEVE JOBS 1955 – 2011

I am the master
of my fate:
I am the captain
of my soul.

WILLIAM ERNEST HENLEY 1849 – 1903

You are not Cleopatra.

Or Marie Curie.

Or Beyoncé.

Or Queen Elizabeth.

You are you. Irreplaceable.

Loved and needed.

Utterly unique.

CHARLOTTE GRAY

The easiest thing in the world
to be is you.
The most difficult thing to be
is what other people
want you to be.
Don't let them put you
in that position.

LEO BUSCAGLIA 1924 – 1998

Y̲ou are utterly unique.
You have something to give
that no one else can give.
It may seem insignificant
but it may change a heart, a mind, a life
Recognize your worth.

HANNAH C. KLEIN

Keep shining. The worl

...eeds your light.

AUTHOR UNKNOWN

A million, million lives
and not one of them you.
You are a unique masterpiece
in Time and Space.

ODILE DORMEUIL

Hold your head high, stick your chest out. You can make it.

JESSE JACKSON, B. 1941

To be yourself
in a world that is constantly
trying to make you something else
is the greatest achievement.

RALPH WALDO EMERSON 1803 – 1882

If I am not good to myself,
how can I expect
anyone else to be good to me?

MAYA ANGELOU 1928 – 2014

We will get out of life only
what we work to achieve.
You may have a burning desire to become
a writer, a performer, a doctor or an
entrepreneur… You must choose to
take action. You must choose to discipline
yourself, to stretch yourself and launch
your dreams. Don't look for miracles
to change bad habits. There is no miracle
that will change us…
We must choose to change, to act in our
own behalf.

SUSAN L. TAYLOR, B. 1946

You have brains in your head.
You have feet in your shoes.
You can steer yourself
in any direction you choose.
You're on your own.
And you know what you know.
You are the one
who'll decide where to go.

DR. SEUSS 1904 – 1991

Be a bigger

yourself.

TYRA BANKS, B. 1973

Consider the bear who never roared,
or the eagle who never soared,
or the fern who never opened.
Tap your *Mash-ka-wisen* [inner strength],
walk through your fear,
and embrace your values.
Be who you are!

BLACKWOLF (ROBERT JONES) OJIBWE,
AND GINA JONES

There is nothing you can't do
if you put your mind to it
and believe in yourself.
You just have to listen
to your own drummer
and not somebody else's.

DEREK BEEVOR, B. 1955

I am too intelligent,
too demanding,
and too resourceful for anyone
to be able to
take charge of me entirely.
No one knows me
or loves me completely.
I have only myself

SIMONE DE BEAUVOIR 1908 – 1986

Trust yourself.
Think for yourself.
Act for yourself.
Speak for yourself.
Be yourself.

MARVA COLLINS 1936 – 2015

There are so many different
walks of life,
so many different personalities
in the world.
And no longer do you have to be
a chameleon and try and adapt
to that environment –
you can truly be yourself.

HOPE SOLO, B. 1981

Fashion is what you adopt
when you don't know who you are.

QUENTIN CRISP 1908 – 1999

You were
born
an original.
Don't die
a copy.

JOHN MASON

I got my own back.

MAYA ANGELOU 1928 – 2014

Don't you ever let
a soul in the world
tell you that you can't be
exactly who you are.

LADY GAGA, B. 1986

Be faithful
to that
which exists
nowhere
but in yourself.

ANDRÉ GIDE 1861 – 1951

If I could give one tip for people –
it's not an exercise
or nutrition regimen. It's to
walk your talk
and believe in yourself,
because at the end of the day,
the dumbbell and diet
don't get you in shape.
It's your accountability to your word.

BRETT HOEBEL

In a universe that is infinite,

there is not another you.

You are special.

You are unique.

What a wondrous achievement –

a miracle.

Be proud of yourself.

LINDA GIBSON

Find who you are in this world
and what you need
to feel good alone.
I think that's the most
important thing in life.
Find a sense of self
because with that,
you can do anything else.

ANGELINA JOLIE, B. 1975

Everyone has inside them
a piece of good news!
The good news is that you really
don't know how great you can be,
how much you can love,
and what your potential is!

ANNE FRANK 1929 – 1945

Be yourself.
The world worships
the original.

INGRID BERGMAN 1915 – 1982

If we did all the things
we are capable of doing,
we would literally
astound ourselves.

THOMAS EDISON 1847 – 1931

The formula of happiness
and success is just
being actually yourself, in the most
vivid possible way you can.

MERYL STREEP, B. 1949

None exactly like you
has existed
in all time.
You have something to give
that no one else can give.

ODILE DORMEUIL

I took a deep breath
and listened
to the old brag
of my heart.
I am, I am, I am.

SYLVIA PLATH 1932 – 1963

Just don't give up trying to do what you really want to do.

ELLA FITZGERALD 1917 – 1996

You may be
the only person left
who believes in you,
but it's enough.
It takes just one star
to pierce a universe
of darkness.
Never give up.

RICHELLE E. GOODRICH

You alone are enough.

MAYA ANGELOU 1928 – 2014

Believe in yourself.
You are braver than you think,
more talented than you know,
and capable of more than
you imagine.

ROY T. BENNETT

Just be yourself.
There is no one better.

TAYLOR SWIFT, B. 1989

Believe in love.

Believe in magic.

Believe in yourself.

Believe in your dreams.

If you don't,

who will?

JON BON JOVI, B. 1962

Sparkle!

Hair and make-up, yes.

Shoes and clothes, of course.

But best of all

be yourself.

Your wonderful, marvellous self.

Delight us with your smile!

HANNAH C. KLEIN

You are you.

And what could be better?

A one-off.

A mind and heart that's never been before.

CHARLOTTE GRAY

I'm gonna look back on my life and say that I enjoyed it and I lived it for me.

RIHANNA, B. 1988

W̲e ask ourselves,
"Who am I to be brilliant, gorgeous,
talented, fabulous?"
Actually, who are you not to be?

MARIANNE WILLIAMSON, B. 1952

S̲elf-confidence is the first requisite
to great undertakings.

DR. SAMUEL JOHNSON 1709 – 1784

Carpenters
bend wood;
fletchers
bend arrows;
wise people
fashion
themselves.

GAUTAMA BUDDHA c.563 B.C. – 483 B.C.

It is time for every one of us
to roll up our sleeves
and put ourselves at the top
of our commitment list.

MARIAN WRIGHT EDELMAN, B. 1939

Start where you are.
Use what you have.
Do what you can.

ARTHUR ASHE 1943 – 1993

Follow you

I have an everyday belief
that works for me.
Love yourself first
and everything falls into line.

LUCILLE BALL 1910 – 1989

When you know yourself
you are empowered.
When you accept yourself
you are invincible.

TINA LIFFORD

own star.

DANTE ALIGHIERI 1265 – 1321

When I was young,
I thought confidence could be earned
with perfection. Now I know
that you don't earn it; you claim it.
And you do that by loving the wacky,
endlessly optimistic, enthusiastically
uninhibited free spirit
that is the essence of style,
the quintessence
of heart, and uniquely you.

CECELIE BARRY

It wasn't until I found
the courage to look
in the mirror
and say, "I Love You"
with conviction
that I felt truly amazing!

R.S. LEWIS

And I decided to love myself.

QUEEN LATIFAH, B. 1970

Pursue, keep up with,

circle round and round your life,

as a dog does his master's chaise.

Do what you love.

Know your own bone,

gnaw at it, bury it,

unearth it, and gnaw it still.

HENRY DAVID THOREAU 1817 – 1862

I think everybody's weird. We should all celebrate our individuality and not be embarrassed or ashamed of it.

JOHNNY DEPP, B. 1963

I will not let anyone
walk through
my mind
with their dirty feet.

MAHATMA GANDHI 1869 – 1948

Always be a first-rate
version of yourself,
and not a second-rate version
of someone else.

JUDY GARLAND 1922 – 1969

Believe in yourself.
Pick a path that you,
deep down in your soul,
won't be ashamed of.

HIROMU ARAKAWA, B. 1973

*Find out
who you are and do it
on purpose.*

DOLLY PARTON, B. 1946

Believe in yourself.
You can do it.

SIR RICHARD BRANSON, B. 1950

Dare to love yourself
as if you were a rainbow
with gold at both ends.

ABERJHANI, B. 1957

When there is
no enemy within,
the enemies outside
cannot hurt you.

AFRICAN PROVERB

Our ordinary mind always tries
to persuade us that we are nothing
but acorns and that our
greatest happiness will be
to become bigger, fatter,
shinier acorns; but that is of interest
only to pigs. Our faith gives knowledge
of something much better;
that we can become oak trees.

E. F. SCHUMACHER 1911 – 1977

There are billions of people
in the world and yet you are
an individual. Unique and special!
You have a right to be safe,
to be nourished and to be loved.
You have the right to be happy.

STUART & LINDA MACFARLANE

*Like yourself,
respect yourself,
enjoy yourself
and accept yourself.*

LETTY COTTIN POGREBIN, B. 1939

The best day of your life
is the one on which you decide
your life is your own.
No apologies or excuses.
No one to lean on, rely on, or blame.
The gift is yours –
it is an amazing journey –
and you alone are responsible
for the quality of it.
This is the day that your life
really begins.

BOB MOAWAB

The most courageous act
is still to think for yourself. Aloud.

COCO CHANEL 1883 – 1971

You are a diamond.
Simply waiting for time and effort
to facet you.

PAM BROWN

No one can make you feel inferior
without your consent.

ELEANOR ROOSEVELT 1884 – 1962

One of the greatest
regrets in life is being
what others
would want you to be,
rather than
being yourself.

SHANNON L. ALDER

You have a right to be exactly who you are.

MICHELLE OBAMA, B. 1964

You change
the world by being yourself.

YOKO ONO, B. 1933

How can you hesitate?
Risk! Risk anything!
Care no more for the opinion of others,
for those voices.
Do the hardest thing on earth for you.
Act for yourself. Face the truth.

KATHERINE MANSFIELD 1888 – 1923

I'm tough, I'm ambitious,
and I know exactly what I want.
If that makes me a B****, Okay.

MADONNA, B. 1958

Put your future
in good hands –
your own.

AUTHOR UNKNOWN

*Never waste your time
trying to
cram yourself into
a skin
that doesn't fit.*

HANNAH C. KLEIN

Tension
is who
you think
you should be,
relaxation
is who
you are.

CHINESE PROVERB

The thing everyone
should realise
is that the key
to happiness is being happy
by yourself
and for yourself.

ELLEN DEGENERES, B. 1958

I never lose sight
of the fact
that just being is fun.

KATHARINE HEPBURN 1907 – 2003

Follow what you love!...
Don't deign to ask what "they"
are looking for out there.
Ask what you have inside.
Follow not your interests,
which change, but what you are
and what you love,
which will and should not change.

GEORGIE ANNE GEYER

Cherish forever what

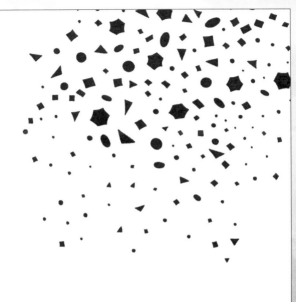

makes you unique.

BETTE MIDLER, B. 1945

I'm not preaching for you to go out
and conquer Mt. Everest,
run the Boston Marathon,
or discover the cure for cancer.
Heck no. But I want you to believe
in yourself, in a certain cause, any cause.
Just believe. To do something,
anything; whether it's taking that one
class at night school, putting down one soda
and walking around

the block once a day,
or taking some loose change now
and then and tossing it into that jar
until it's filled and you have enough
to go out and buy...
you get the idea. Point being:
All achievements,
whether great or small,
take root in the belief
in the act itself.

DAVE PELZER, B. 1960

Only you can control your future.

DR. SEUSS 1904 – 1991

Nothing can dim
the light that shines
from within.

MAYA ANGELOU 1928 – 2014

As soon as you
trust yourself,
you will know
how to live.

JOHANN WOLFGANG VON GOETHE
1749 – 1832

How many cares
one loses
when one decides
not to be something,
but to be someone.

COCO CHANEL 1883 – 1971

I think self-awareness
is the most important thing
toward being a champion.

BILLIE JEAN KING, B. 1943

No bird soars too high,
if he soars with his own wings.

WILLIAM BLAKE 1757 – 1827

Create the kind of self
that you will be happy
to live with all your life

GOLDA MEIR 1898 – 1978

Remember always that you
have not only the right
to be an individual;
you have an obligation to be one.
You cannot make any useful
contribution in life
unless you do this.

ELEANOR ROOSEVELT 1884 – 1962

Go confidently
in the direction
of your dreams!
Live the life
you've imagined.

HENRY DAVID THOREAU 1817 – 1862

Doubt is a killer.
You just have to know
who you are
and what you stand for.

JENNIFER LOPEZ, B. 1970

Be unapologetically
you.

STEVE MARABOLI, B. 1975

Wear your dreams like diamonds.

STUART & LINDA MACFARLANE

Without you there
would be a hole
in the Universe.

PAMELA DUGDALE

*You are
what you believe
yourself to be.*

PAULO COELHO, B. 1947

When someone tells you
that you are different,
smile and hold your head up
and be proud

ANGELINA JOLIE, B. 1975

Life isn't about
finding yourself.
Life is about
creating yourself.

GEORGE BERNARD SHAW 1856 – 1950

Trust thyself:
every heart vibrates
to that iron string.

RALPH WALDO EMERSON
1803 – 1882

The highest courage
is to dare
to appear to be what one is.

JOHN LANCASTER SPALDING
c.1609 – 1670

I just want you to be yourself.

TYRA BANKS, B. 1973

Tiny, little you –
the most important person
in the universe –
How wonderful is that?

STUART & LINDA MACFARLANE

No other version,
no matter how perfect it is,
would feel better than
being your true self.

EDMOND MBIAKA

The things that make me different are the things that make me.

A. A. MILNE 1882 – 1956

There is just one life fo

Don't compare yourself
with anyone in this world...
If you do so,
you are insulting yourself.

BILL GATES, B. 1955

each of us: our own.

EURIPIDES c.480 B.C. – 406 B.C.

Your self-worth
is defined by you.
You don't have to depend on
someone telling you who you are.

BEYONCÉ, B. 1981

We need to learn
to love ourselves first,
in all our glory
and our imperfections.

JOHN LENNON 1940 – 1980